D1743616

Claire's

C·O·N·S·E·R·V·E·S·

—AND PRESERVES—

CLAIRE ATTRIDGE

Macdonald Orbis

A *Macdonald Orbis* Book

First published in Great Britain in 1987
by Macdonald & Co (Publishers) Ltd
London & Sydney

A member of BPCC plc

Conceived, designed and produced by
The Albion Press Ltd
P.O. Box 52, Princes Risborough, Aylesbury, Bucks., HP17 9PR

Editor: Jo Christian
Consultant: Jan Buck
Designer: Linda Sullivan

British Library Cataloguing in Publication Data
Attridge, Claire
Claire's conserves and preserves.—— (Claire's kitchen).
1. Cookery (Chutney)   2. Pickles   3. Fruit preservation
I. Title   II. Series   641.6'16   TX805
ISBN 0–356–14874–2

Typeset by Wyvern Typesetting Ltd, Bristol
Colour origination by Culver Graphics Litho Ltd
Printed and bound in Italy by New Interlitho

Macdonald & Co (Publishers) Ltd

Greater London House Hampstead Road London NW1 7QX

· CONTENTS ·

· INTRODUCTION ·

In this book you will find out how to make delicious jams, marmalades, curds and preserved fruits, along with pickles, chutneys and flavoured vinegars and oils. All these preserves have been chosen to be simple to make and easy to keep, needing no special expertise or expensive equipment.

Equipment, cooking and testing   There are a few tips, however, which will help you make the best of your time and your ingredients. Always make jams in a big pan — it should be wide and deep, so that the ingredients come to no more than half-way up the sides. This allows plenty of space for the jam to bubble, without the risk of boiling over and getting burnt on to your cooker top. Heavy aluminium or stainless steel pans are the best to use. Any pan used for making preserves should have a heavy base, to prevent burning, especially when you are cooking thick mixtures with little liquid, such as chutneys.

As the jam mixture heats, the sugar starts to dissolve. It is essential that you begin with a gentle heat, and make sure that all the sugar does dissolve before you turn the heat up and boil the mixture to cook it. If any sugar crystals remain undissolved in the mixture, they may turn the entire batch of finished jam sugary.

If you already have a sugar thermometer, you may find it useful, but it is hardly worth buying one specially — thermometers are hard to read when they are covered in jam! The following simple test is perfectly adequate for checking whether jams and marmalades are cooked enough to set properly. Remove the pan from the heat, and put a small spoonful of jam on to a cold saucer. Leave it for a minute or two to cool — you can put the saucer in the fridge or freezer to speed this up. When the jam is cold, push it gently with the tip of your finger: if it is firm enough to wrinkle, the jam is ready to set. If it is still too runny, return the pan to the heat for a few minutes, then do the same test again.

To make a clear fruit jelly (page 26), juice has to be strained through a jelly bag into a bowl underneath. If you haven't got a jelly bag you can improvise: take a large square of muslin, fold it to give several thicknesses, and tie the four corners to the legs of an upturned stool. But, really, it is much easier to buy a jelly bag! They are available at all good kitchen shops, and are not expensive.

No special tips are needed for chutneys, other than to make sure that you do not overcook them. The times given in the recipes are a good guide, along with your own judgement of the mixture's thickness and softness. If you are in doubt, err on the side of leaving the chutney a bit thinner than you'd like — chutneys thicken a good bit more as they cool.

Storage   When you have gone to the trouble of making your own preserves, the last thing you want is for them to be spoilt in the keeping. So you must make absolutely sure that you store and cover them properly.

You can use jars of virtually any shape or size, though you should of course make sure that they have no chips or cracks. Wash the jars in warm, soapy water and rinse and dry them carefully. Before you fill jars with a hot preserve, warm them in a low oven (140°C/ 275°F/gas mark 1) and fill them when they are hot — if a hot mixture is put into a cold jar, the glass may crack.

The surface of a sugar conserve or a chutney should be sealed with a waxed paper disc. The easiest to use are ready-cut discs which are sold specially for covering home-made jams. If you are not using standard jars, you can cut your own waxed paper to fit the necks of your jars.

When you have poured the preserve into the jar, while it is still very hot, put the waxed paper disc on top, waxed side down. Run your finger lightly over it to make sure it lies absolutely flat, with all the air excluded. To finish covering a sugar conserve, damp one side of a piece of cellophane and stretch it, damp side up, over the mouth of the jar. Secure it with a rubber band under the rim. Or you can just stretch a piece of clingfilm over the neck of the jar.

Cellophane covers are not suitable for chutneys. All vinegar and alcohol preserves need completely airtight covers, or the liquid will evaporate during storage. For all these preserves, it is simplest to use jars or bottles that have plastic-lined screw tops or tight-fitting corks. Line corks with greaseproof paper to prevent evaporation. Avoid metal lids, as the metal may react with the vinegar or alcohol.

Store all preserves in a cool, dry and preferably dark place, for example inside a cupboard or a pantry. Strong light will reduce the keeping qualities of preserves and may cause discoloration of delicate fruits. Most of the preserves in this book will keep well for at least a year, and by that time the raw materials for another batch should be in season and at their cheapest.

Further reading   If you are interested in more advanced preserve-making, there are several reliable books that cover the subject well. These include: Marye Cameron-Smith, *The Complete Book of Preserving* (Marshall Cavendish, 1976); Good Housekeeping Institute, *The Good Housekeeping Complete Book of Home Preserving* (Ebury Press, 1981); Jocasta Innes, *The Country Kitchen* (Frances Lincoln, 1979); Ministry of Agriculture, Fisheries and Food, *Home Preservation of Fruit and Vegetables* (Her Majesty's Stationery Office, 1971); *Preserving* (The Good Cook Series, Time-Life Books, 1980), and Delia Smith, *Delia Smith's Complete Cookery Course* (BBC Publications, 1978).

*1.75kg/4lb small, firm
    strawberries, hulled and
    wiped, but not washed
1.5kg/3½lb sugar
125ml/4fl oz lemon juice*

Makes about 2.75kg/6lb

Layer the strawberries in a bowl, sprinkling each layer with the sugar. Cover the bowl with a clean cloth and leave overnight: the sugar will draw out the juice, making the berries firmer so that they stay whole when they are cooked.

Wash and rinse the jam jars well and put them in a low oven (140°C/275°F/gas mark 1) to warm. Transfer the contents of the bowl to a preserving pan or a large saucepan and set the pan, uncovered, over a low heat. Shake the pan from time to time to stop the mixture from sticking. When the sugar has dissolved, add the lemon juice, turn up the heat and bring the jam to the boil. Boil rapidly for 5 minutes, then test for setting. Either use a sugar thermometer, or take the pan off the heat, put a teaspoon of jam on a cold saucer and leave it to cool: if it is firm enough to wrinkle when you push it with your fingertip, the jam is ready to set (see page 9). If it is still runny, put the pan back on the heat and boil for another 2 or 3 minutes, then test again. Continue boiling and testing till the jam reaches setting point.

When the jam is ready, skim any froth from the top with a metal spoon. Leave the jam for 15 minutes to settle and cool slightly, then stir it very gently to make sure the fruit is evenly distributed. Ladle the jam into the warmed jars, filling each one to within 1cm/½inch of the top. Cover the surface of the jam in each jar immediately with a waxed paper disc, waxed side down. Run a finger over the surface of the disc to make sure it sits snugly on top of the jam, with all the air excluded. Damp a piece of cellophane on one side only, and stretch it, damp side up, over the mouth of the jar (when it dries it will be taut and smooth). Secure it with a rubber band. Use a hot, damp cloth to wipe any drips or stickiness off the jars. Label them when they are cold.

900g/2lb blackcurrants,
washed, stalks removed
600ml/1pint water
1.25kg/3lb sugar

Makes about 2.25kg/5lb

Put the blackcurrants with the water in a preserving pan or a large saucepan. Set the pan over a low heat and simmer slowly, stirring from time to time, for about 45 minutes, till the skins of the blackcurrants are soft.

Meanwhile, warm the sugar for 15 minutes in a moderate oven (180°C/350°F/gas mark 4). When the fruit is tender, stir in the warmed sugar. Turn the oven down to 140°C/275°F/gas mark 1 and, when the temperature has dropped, put in the jam jars to warm. Cook the jam gently, stirring often, for about 15 minutes, till all the sugar has melted. Turn up the heat, bring the jam to the boil and boil it fast, stirring occasionally, for 5 minutes. Test for setting with a sugar thermometer, or take the pan from the heat and test a spoonful of jam on a saucer (see page 9). Continue boiling and testing the jam until the setting point is reached.

Remove any froth from the surface of the jam with a metal spoon. Leave the jam to settle for 15 minutes, stir it to distribute the fruit evenly, then ladle it into the warmed jars. Cover the jars at once (see page 10). Label them when they are cold.

*1.25kg/3lb gooseberries,
    topped, tailed and washed
5 or 6 elderflower heads
1.25litres/2pints water*

1.75kg/4lb sugar

Makes about 2.75 kg/6 lb

[You will also need a piece of muslin at least 25cm/10inches
square and some string.]

Tie up the elderflowers in the piece of muslin. Put them in a
preserving pan with the gooseberries and the water and simmer
for about 30 minutes, till the gooseberries are soft and the
contents of the pan are reduced by about a third. Meanwhile,
warm the sugar for 15 minutes in a moderate oven (180°C/
350°F/gas mark 4). Take out the elderflowers, stir in the
warmed sugar and cook slowly, stirring often, till the sugar has
dissolved. Turn up the heat and boil hard, stirring from time to
time, for 15 minutes. Test for setting (see page 9). If necessary,
continue to boil and test till setting point is reached. Remove
any froth from the surface. Leave the jam to settle for 15
minutes, ladle it into warmed jars and cover it (see page 10).

· APRICOT JAM ·

1.25kg/3lb apricots, washed,
  halved, stones removed
juice of 1 lemon
300ml/½pint water

1.25kg/3lb sugar
50g/2oz almonds, blanched
  and split
Makes about 2.25kg/5lb

Put the apricots in a preserving pan, add the lemon juice and
the water and simmer for 15 minutes or so, till the fruit is soft.
At the same time, warm the sugar for 15 minutes in a
moderate oven (180°C/350°F/gas mark 4). Stir the almonds and
the warmed sugar into the fruit. Cook the mixture over a low
heat, stirring frequently, till the sugar has dissolved. Turn up
the heat and boil the jam, stirring occasionally, for 15 minutes.
Test for setting (see page 9). If necessary, continue to boil and
test till the setting point is reached. Remove any froth from the
surface. Leave the jam to settle for 15 minutes, then stir to
distribute the fruit and the almonds evenly. Ladle the jam into
warmed jars and cover it (see page 10).

· SEVILLE ORANGE MARMALADE ·

900g/2lb Seville oranges,
  washed   *1.75kg/4lb sugar*
1 lemon, washed
2.25litres/4pints water   Makes about 2.75kg/6lb
[You will also need a piece of muslin at least 25cm/10inches
square and some string.]

Cut the oranges and the lemon in half; squeeze out the juice
and pour it into a preserving pan. Scoop the pulp and all the
pips out of the fruit, put them on the muslin, and tie it to
make a bag. Cut the fruit peel, with the pith, into shreds —
thick or thin, depending on how you like your marmalade. If
you want a chunky marmalade use all the peel; otherwise
discard some. Add the peel, the muslin bag and the water to
the juice in the pan.

Bring the liquid just to the boil over a medium heat, then
turn the heat low and simmer for about 2 hours, till the peel is
tender and the contents of the pan are reduced by about half.
Warm the sugar for 15 minutes in a moderate oven (180°C/
350°F/gas mark 4). Remove the muslin bag from the pan and
squeeze it to extract all the jelly, which is rich in the setting
agent pectin. Stir this jelly into the marmalade mixture and tip
in the warmed sugar. Continue to cook over a low heat, stirring
frequently, till all the sugar has dissolved.

Turn the heat up high, bring the marmalade to the boil and
boil hard, stirring occasionally, for 15 minutes. Test for setting
(see page 9). If necessary, continue to boil and test at 5-minute
intervals till the setting point is reached. Skim the marmalade
and leave it to settle for 15 minutes, then stir it to distribute
the peel evenly. Ladle the marmalade into warmed jars. Cover
the jars at once (see page 10) and label them when cold.

· THREE-FRUIT MARMALADE ·

2 lemons, washed   Makes about 2kg/4½lb
1 sweet orange, washed
1 grapefruit, washed
1.75litres/3pints water
1.25kg/3lb sugar
[You will also need a piece of muslin at least 25cm/10inches
square and some string.]

Using a sharp knife or a vegetable peeler, pare the rind thinly
from the fruits and slice it into fine shreds. Peel the pith off the
fruits, and put it on the muslin. Chop the flesh roughly on a
plate, keeping all the juice. Take out the pips as you go and put
them on the muslin with the pith. Tie the muslin into a bag.
Put the peel, the chopped fruit, the juice, the muslin bag and
the water into a preserving pan.

   Bring the liquid just to the boil and simmer for about 1½
hours, till the peel is soft and the contents of the pan are
reduced by half. Warm the sugar for 15 minutes in a moderate
oven (180°C/350°F/gas mark 4). Take the muslin bag from the
pan and squeeze it to extract the jelly. Stir the jelly into the
marmalade mixture. Add the sugar to the mixture in the pan

20

and cook over a low heat, stirring frequently, till it has all dissolved. Then bring the marmalade to the boil and boil rapidly, stirring from time to time, for 15 minutes. Test for setting (see page 9). If necessary, continue to boil and test at 5-minute intervals till the setting point is reached.

Remove any froth with a metal spoon, then leave the marmalade to cool for 15 minutes. Stir to distribute the peel. Ladle the marmalade into warmed jars. Cover the jars (see page 10) and wipe them with a hot, damp cloth. Label them when they are cold.

Grapefruit and Lemon Marmalade   Follow the same method as for three-fruit marmalade, using 3 grapefruit and 4 lemons to 1.75litres/3pints of water and 1.25kg/3lb of sugar.

Ginger Marmalade   Add about 175g/6oz of chopped crystallized ginger, or ginger that has been preserved in syrup, to three-fruit marmalade or grapefruit and lemon marmalade, stirring it in with the sugar. For a richer flavour and a darker colour, you can use Demerara sugar.

· LEMON CURD ·

juice and thinly pared rind of
  6 large lemons
350g/12oz butter, cut in little
  pieces

900g/2lb caster sugar
8 eggs, beaten

Makes about 1.25kg/3lb

Lemon curd is very easy to make, as long as the heat is kept low. The mixture must not come to the boil, or it will curdle.

Put all the ingredients in a bowl set over a saucepan of simmering water, or in the top of a double boiler. Cook, stirring, till the butter has melted and the sugar has completely dissolved. Take the bowl from the heat and strain the mixture through a nylon sieve into another bowl. Discard the lemon rind. Put the strained mixture, in a clean bowl, back on top of the pan of hot water or pour it into the cleaned top of the double boiler. Continue to cook, stirring frequently, till the curd is thick enough to coat the back of a wooden spoon. This may take 40 minutes, or even longer.

Ladle the curd into dry, warmed jars. Cover the surface of the curd in each jar with a waxed paper disc, then cover the jars (see page 10). Label them when they are cold.

Lemon curd is delicious used as a spread, as a filling for tarts or to sandwich the two halves of a sponge cake. Orange curd makes a pleasant and more unusual alternative.

Orange Curd   You can make orange curd in the same way as lemon curd, substituting the rind and juice of 5 medium oranges for the lemons. If you like a fairly sharp taste, add the juice of half a lemon to the orange juice.

*Note   These curds do not keep as long as jams. Store them in a cool place, or in the fridge, and use them within 3 months.

350g/12oz sultanas
350g/12oz raisins
350g/12oz currants
225g/8oz chopped mixed peel
225g/8oz almonds, blanched
  and slivered
225g/8oz cooking apples,
  peeled, cored and grated
225g/8oz Barbados or
  Demerara sugar
225g/8oz beef suet, finely
  chopped

1 teaspoon ground cinnamon
1 teaspoon grated nutmeg
2 teaspoons ground mixed
  spice
juice and finely grated rind of
  1 large lemon
juice and finely grated rind of
  1 medium orange
150ml/¼pint brandy

Makes about 2.25kg/5lb

Put all the ingredients except the fruit juice and brandy in a large bowl and mix them together very thoroughly. Stir in the fruit juice and then the brandy, then spoon the mixture into clean, dry jars. Cover the surface of the mincemeat in each jar with a waxed paper disc, then cover and label the jars (see pages 10–11). Store the mincemeat in a cool, dark place. It should be allowed to mature for 4 weeks before it is used, and will keep well for at least a year. If it becomes dry during storage, stir in a little more brandy.

Mincemeat is, of course, best known as the filling for the mince pies that are eaten at Christmas time, but it is also excellent sandwiched between two layers of shortbread. It makes a good topping for a tart, or basis for a crumble as well. All of these are delectable served with brandy butter.

Brandy Butter Cream together 100g/4oz unsalted butter and 100g/4oz caster or icing sugar. Beat in, a few drops at a time, 4 tablespoons of brandy. Spoon the brandy butter into little pots,

cover them and chill for 2 or 3 hours before serving. Covered,
brandy butter will keep in the fridge for 2 weeks.

*1.75kg/4lb cooking apples,
washed and roughly
chopped*
peel of 1 lemon

about 1.75litres/3pints water
about 700g/1½lb sugar

Makes about 1.5kg/3½lb

Put the chopped apples and the lemon peel in a preserving pan and add enough water to cover the fruit. Bring to the boil, then simmer, uncovered, stirring occasionally, for about half an hour, till the fruit is pulpy and the liquid is reduced by about a third. Tip the purée into a jelly bag over a large bowl and leave it overnight for the juice to strain through. Discard the lemon peel and the apple pulp remaining in the bag. Measure the juice into a preserving pan and add 450g/1lb of sugar for every 600ml/1pint of juice. Cook over a low heat till the sugar has dissolved, then boil hard for 10 to 20 minutes, till the setting point is reached (see page 9). Remove any froth, ladle the jelly into warmed jars and cover them (see page 10). Label them when cold.

Plain apple jelly is an excellent spread for bread or scones. With the addition of different herbs, it becomes an appetising accompaniment for meat or fish.

Mint Jelly   Simmer a small bunch of mint with the apples. After straining, discard it with the pulp remaining in the jelly bag. Add a couple of tablespoons of freshly chopped mint to each jar when you bottle the jelly.

Rosemary or Thyme Jelly   Simmer some sprigs of the herb with the apples. Discard after straining and replace with fresh sprigs when you bottle the jelly.

Sage or Dill Jelly   Put a sprig of the herb into each jar of jelly.

· SPICED ORANGE RINGS ·

900g/2lb thin-skinned
  oranges, washed
1 teaspoon each allspice
  berries, coriander seeds and
  whole cloves
5cm/2inch stick cinnamon,
  broken in pieces

450g/1lb sugar
425ml/¾pint white wine
  vinegar

Makes about 900g/2lb

[You will also need a small piece of muslin and some string.]

Slice the oranges into rings about 5mm/¼inch thick. Place the slices in a large pan and pour in enough water to cover them. Bring the liquid to the boil, put the lid on the pan and simmer for about 45 minutes, till the peel of the oranges is soft.

Meanwhile, tie all the spices up in a piece of muslin and crush them lightly with a pestle or a rolling pin. Put the sugar in another large pan with the vinegar and cook gently, stirring often, till the sugar has dissolved. Add the spice bag, bring to the boil and boil for a minute or two. Use a slotted spoon to transfer the orange slices to the spiced syrup (keep their cooking water for the time being). There should be just enough liquid to cover the fruit — if necessary, top up the syrup with some of the water the oranges were cooked in. Simmer, with the lid on the pan, for half an hour. Then transfer the oranges, with the syrup and spice bag, to a bowl, cover it with a clean cloth and leave overnight.

The next day, pour the fruit and the syrup back into the clean pan and bring to the boil. Lift out the oranges with the slotted spoon, and pack them in warmed jars. Bring the syrup back to the boil, and boil it uncovered for a few minutes, till it begins to thicken. Discard the spice bag and pour the syrup over the orange slices. Cover the jars with a screw top or cork (see page 11) and keep them in a cool, dark place for about 6

weeks for their flavour to mature. They make a lovely
accompaniment to hot or cold roast poultry, especially duck,
and to cold ham.

*700g/1½lb small pickling
    onions*
1.75litres/3pints water
175g/6oz sea salt
425ml/¾pint malt vinegar
5cm/2inch stick cinnamon

*1 tablespoon each blade mace
    and allspice berries*
5 or 6 peppercorns
1 bay leaf

Makes about 900g/2lb

Put the onions, unpeeled, in a large bowl. Bring half the water
to the boil and dissolve half the salt in it. Pour this brine over
the onions. To make sure the onions are kept under the liquid,
put a plate on top and weigh it down with a small weight.
Leave overnight, then drain and peel the onions. Dissolve the
rest of the salt in the remaining water to make fresh brine.
Pour it over the onions and leave them for another 24 hours.

   Put the vinegar with the spices and the bay leaf in a
saucepan. Bring the liquid to the boil and pour it into a jug (not
a metal one). Cover and leave for 2 hours. Strain the spiced
vinegar through muslin or a fine-meshed nylon sieve. Drain and
rinse the onions, pack them into jars and pour in the spiced
vinegar. Cover the jars (see page 11) and label them.

*900g/2lb button mushrooms,
trimmed and wiped
1 small onion, peeled and
finely chopped
900ml/1½pints malt vinegar*

*2 teaspoons salt
1 teaspoon freshly ground
black or white pepper
4 blades mace*
Makes about 1.25kg/3lb

Put all the ingredients except the mushrooms into a large pan.
Bring the liquid to the boil, then add the mushrooms and
simmer over a low heat for about 10 minutes, till the
mushrooms are soft and have shrunk a little. Spoon the
mushrooms into warmed jars and pour the hot vinegar and
spices over them. Cover the jars at once (see page 11), and label
them when they are cold.

* Store both these pickles in a cool, dry, dark place and leave
them to mature for 2 or 3 months. They are very good served
with cold meat, or bread, cheese and salad.

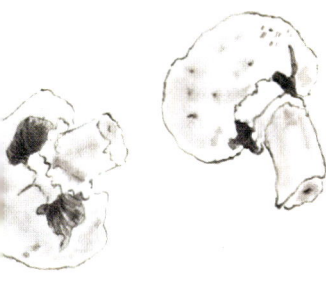
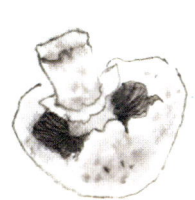
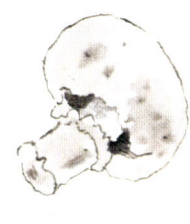

900g/2lb green peppers,
  washed, seeded and sliced
450g/1lb tomatoes, peeled
  and chopped
450g/1lb onions, peeled and
  sliced
450g/1lb apples, peeled, cored
  and chopped

175g/6oz Barbados or
  Demerara sugar
1 teaspoon each allspice
  berries, black peppercorns
  and mustard seeds
425ml/¾pint malt vinegar

Makes about 1.5kg/3½lb

[You will also need a small piece of muslin and some string.]

Put all the ingredients except the spices and the malt vinegar in a preserving pan. Tie the spices up in the muslin and crush them lightly. Put the spice bag in the pan and pour over the vinegar. Cook over a low heat till the sugar has dissolved, then bring the mixture gently to the boil and simmer over a medium heat, stirring frequently to stop the chutney sticking to the pan. The chutney is ready when it has a soft, thick consistency and almost all the vinegar has been absorbed — after about 1¾ hours. Take out the spice bag, ladle the chutney into warmed jars and cover (see page 11).

900g/2lb aubergines, washed and sliced
3 tablespoons salt
1 medium onion, peeled and finely chopped
5 sticks celery, washed and finely chopped
100g/4oz sultanas

3 cloves garlic, peeled and crushed
175g/6oz Barbados or Demerara sugar
1 teaspoon cayenne pepper
350ml/12fl oz malt vinegar

Makes about 1.25kg/3lb

Layer the aubergine slices in a colander, sprinkling each layer with salt, and put a weighted plate on top. Leave them for about an hour for the bitter juices to drain, then rinse and dry them. Put them in a preserving pan with all the other ingredients. Cook over a low heat till the sugar has dissolved, then bring the mixture to the boil. Simmer over a medium heat, stirring frequently, for about 1½ hours, till the chutney is soft and thick. Ladle it into warmed jars and cover them (see page 11).

* Leave both these chutneys for about 3 months for their flavour to mature. Serve them with cold meats and curries.

1.25kg/3lb gooseberries,
    topped, tailed and washed
1 medium onion, peeled and
    finely chopped
350g/12oz sugar
225g/8oz sultanas

1 tablespoon salt
2 teaspoons ground ginger
1 teaspoon cayenne pepper
600ml/1pint malt vinegar

Makes about 1.75kg/4lb

Boil the chopped onion in a little water till it is soft. Drain it and put it in a preserving pan with all the other ingredients. Cook over a low heat till the sugar has dissolved, then bring the mixture slowly to the boil and simmer over a medium heat, stirring frequently, till most of the liquid has evaporated and the chutney is soft and thick — about 1 hour. Ladle the chutney into warmed jars and cover it immediately (see page 11). Leave it to mature for about 3 months. Gooseberry chutney makes a tangy accompaniment to oily fish such as mackerel.

· PEAR CHUTNEY ·

*1.25kg/3lb pears, peeled,
  cored and chopped
450g/1lb onions, peeled and
  finely chopped
450g/1lb sultanas
450g/1lb Barbados or
  Demerara sugar*

*2 teaspoons salt
25g/1oz ground ginger
1 tablespoon mustard powder
1.25litres/2pints malt vinegar*

Makes about 1.75kg/4lb

Put all the ingredients in a preserving pan. Cook over a low
heat till the sugar has dissolved. Bring the mixture to the boil
and then simmer gently, stirring fairly often, for about $2\frac{1}{2}$
hours, till the chutney is thick and brown. Ladle the chutney
into warmed jars and cover it immediately (see page 11). Leave
it to mature for about 3 months. This chutney is a good
accompaniment to cold meats, especially pork.

35

several bunches of fresh
herbs, washed
3litres/5pints cider vinegar, or
white or red wine vinegar

Makes 3litres/5pints

With herb vinegar you can easily add a special flavour to your cooking. Tarragon vinegar is widely available, but other herb vinegars are difficult or impossible to buy.

Put bunches of herbs such as thyme, sage, tarragon, marjoram, basil, dill or parsley into glass jars or bottles, packing them either individually or in combinations of different herbs. A mixture of tarragon, thyme, parsley and marjoram makes a useful mixed herb vinegar. Fill the jars with good-quality cider vinegar, red or white wine vinegar, stopper them tightly and leave them in a cool place for about 3 weeks. Strain the vinegar through a nylon sieve, pressing the herbs with a wooden spoon to extract as much of their flavour as possible.

Taste the vinegar. If the flavour is not strong enough, start again using fresh herbs, and strain and taste again after a week. If the flavour is too strong, simply add more vinegar. When the herb vinegar is to your liking, pour it into clean bottles. Put a fresh herb sprig into each bottle for decoration. Stopper the bottles.

Herb vinegars make a wonderful addition to salad dressings, mayonnaise, marinades, soups, stews and gravies. Try using tarragon vinegar in a vinaigrette dressing for a chicken salad, or adding a little basil vinegar to tomato soup, thyme vinegar to a marinade for kebabs, marjoram vinegar to gravy for roast beef, or mixed herb vinegar to a stew.

900g/2lb raspberries
1.25litres/2pints white wine
  vinegar
about 700g/1½lb sugar

Makes about 1.75litres/3pints

Put the raspberries in a bowl and crush them lightly with the back of a wooden spoon. Pour the vinegar over them and cover the bowl with a clean cloth. Leave the raspberries soaking in the vinegar for 4 days, stirring them from time to time. Strain the mixture through muslin or a fine-meshed nylon sieve. Measure the quantity of liquid and stir in 225g/8oz of sugar for each 600ml/1pint of liquid. Dissolve the sugar in the vinegar, stirring it over a low heat, then bring the mixture to simmering point and simmer for 10 minutes. Let the raspberry vinegar cool, then bottle it. If you like, put a few whole raspberries in each bottle for decoration. Stopper the bottles tightly and store them in a cool place.

Raspberry vinegar has traditionally been used as a cordial, and a remedy for coughs, colds and sore throats. Diluted with hot water, it makes a soothing drink; with sparkling mineral water, it is pleasantly refreshing. Used in a vinaigrette, it adds a delicious flavour to a salad.

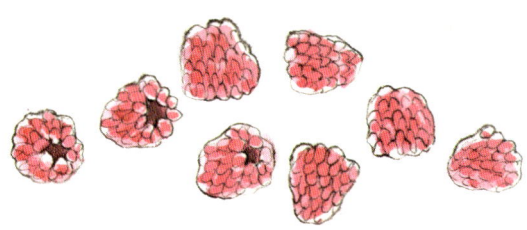

37

· ROSEMARY OIL ·

a bunch of fresh rosemary,   Makes 600ml/1pint
   washed
600ml/1pint mild olive,
   sunflower or safflower oil
[A small piece of muslin.]

Bruise the rosemary lightly, place it in a glass jar and cover it with the oil. Tie a piece of muslin over the mouth of the jar and leave it in a warm, sunny place for about 2 weeks, stirring it once or twice a day. Strain the oil through muslin or a nylon sieve, pressing the rosemary with the back of a wooden spoon to extract the flavour. Taste the oil: if the flavour is not strong enough, repeat the process using fresh rosemary; if it is too strong, top up with more oil. When the oil is to your liking, pour it into clean, dry bottles. Add a fresh sprig of rosemary to each bottle, both to identify it and to decorate it, and stopper the bottles tightly.

Rosemary oil adds a rich, subtle flavour to sauces and salad dressings. Used in marinades and for basting, it imparts its flavour to meat and fish.

Other herb oils can be made in the same way. Tarragon, thyme and oregano oils are all delightful. Basil oil is especially useful in the winter, retaining far more of the flavour of fresh basil than the dried herb does.

· BRANDIED CHERRIES ·

900g/2lb red or black cherries,
* washed*
5cm/2inch stick cinnamon
* (optional)*

450g/1lb sugar
600ml/1pint water
about 300ml/½pint brandy
Makes about 900g/2lb

Choose cherries that are just ripe — if they are at all over-ripe they will become soft during storage. Prick the cherries all over with a needle and arrange them in jars, filling each one to within 1cm/½inch of the top. For extra flavour, you can put a little bit of cinnamon stick in each jar.

Put the sugar in a saucepan with the water and stir over a moderate heat till the sugar dissolves. Stop stirring, bring to the boil and put a warmed sugar thermometer into the syrup. Boil, without stirring, till the temperature reaches 110°C/230°F. Take the syrup off the heat and let it cool, then measure it and add an equal quantity of brandy. Pour the brandied syrup over the cherries and cover the jars securely (see page 11). Put the jars in a cool, dark cupboard and leave the preserve to mature for at least 2 weeks – longer if you can. It improves as it ages, and will keep for several years.

For brandied apricots, peaches or plums, follow the same method. Peel apricots; peel, halve and stone peaches; just prick plums, in the same way as the cherries. Other spirits — gin, whisky, rum or vodka, for example — can be substituted for the brandy.

Fruits preserved in alcohol are a luxurious treat, dessert and liqueur in one, and make very welcome presents.

· ANNEMARIE'S CASSIS ·

*450g/1lb blackcurrants,
washed, stalks removed
600ml/1pint flavourless
vodka*

*225g/8oz sugar
600ml/1pint water*
Makes about 1.5litres/
2½pints

Crush the blackcurrants with a potato masher or the back of a wooden spoon. Put them in a glass jar with an airtight lid and cover them with the vodka. Fasten the lid securely. Put the jar in a warm, bright place (a warm, sunny windowsill is ideal) and leave it for about 3 weeks, shaking it from time to time. Strain the liquid through muslin, or a fine-meshed nylon sieve, pressing gently to extract all the juice.

Put the sugar and water in a saucepan and cook over a moderate heat, stirring frequently, till the sugar has dissolved. Leave the syrup to get quite cold, then mix it with the blackcurrant liquid. Pour the liqueur into bottles and cork them tightly. Leave the cassis for another week, and then you can drink it. However, if you can manage to keep it for a few months, it will taste even better.

The best time to make cassis is when fresh blackcurrants are in season. But you can also make it at any time of year with frozen blackcurrants, though you will need to leave the fruit macerating in the vodka for a week or so longer.

A dash of cassis topped up with dry white wine (preferably white burgundy) makes the delicious aperitif Kir; with sparkling wine (preferably champagne, of course!) it is Kir Royal.

Raspberry Liqueur Using exactly the same method, substitute raspberries for the blackcurrants. Mixed with white wine, this makes Kir Framboise.

Both of these liqueurs are excellent poured over fresh fruit in season, or as sauces for ice cream.

edible flowers, petals or leaves
1 egg white
about 225g/8oz caster sugar

Enough for about 50 rose petals or 20 primroses or violets

Pick flowers and leaves for crystallizing on a sunny morning, when they are quite dry, with no rain or dew on them. You can crystallize small flowers, such as violets, whole; larger flowers, such as roses, should be divided into separate petals.

Line a wire rack with a sheet of greaseproof paper. Whisk the egg white lightly, till it is opaque but not too foamy. Use a soft paintbrush to coat both sides of each flower, petal or leaf with egg white, then sprinkle both sides with caster sugar. Place the coated flowers and leaves in a single layer on the wire rack and cover them with another sheet of greaseproof paper. Put them in a warm airing cupboard or a very low oven with the door ajar, and leave them to dry for about 24 hours.

When they are quite dry and brittle, store them between layers of greaseproof paper in an airtight container. They will keep for about 2 months and make very pretty decorations for cakes, sweets and desserts.

* Note Do make quite sure that the flowers you choose are edible. Try primroses, violets, roses, freesias, apple blossom or cherry blossom, and leaves such as mint or lemon balm.

44